This ACTIVITY BOOK belongs to:

SAY NO to the DUMP

The women in this book dreamed of making our planet a better place. They fought against important issues like pollution, deforestation and global warming by being brave and believing in their ideas. Join these brilliant women and find your power to save the planet too!

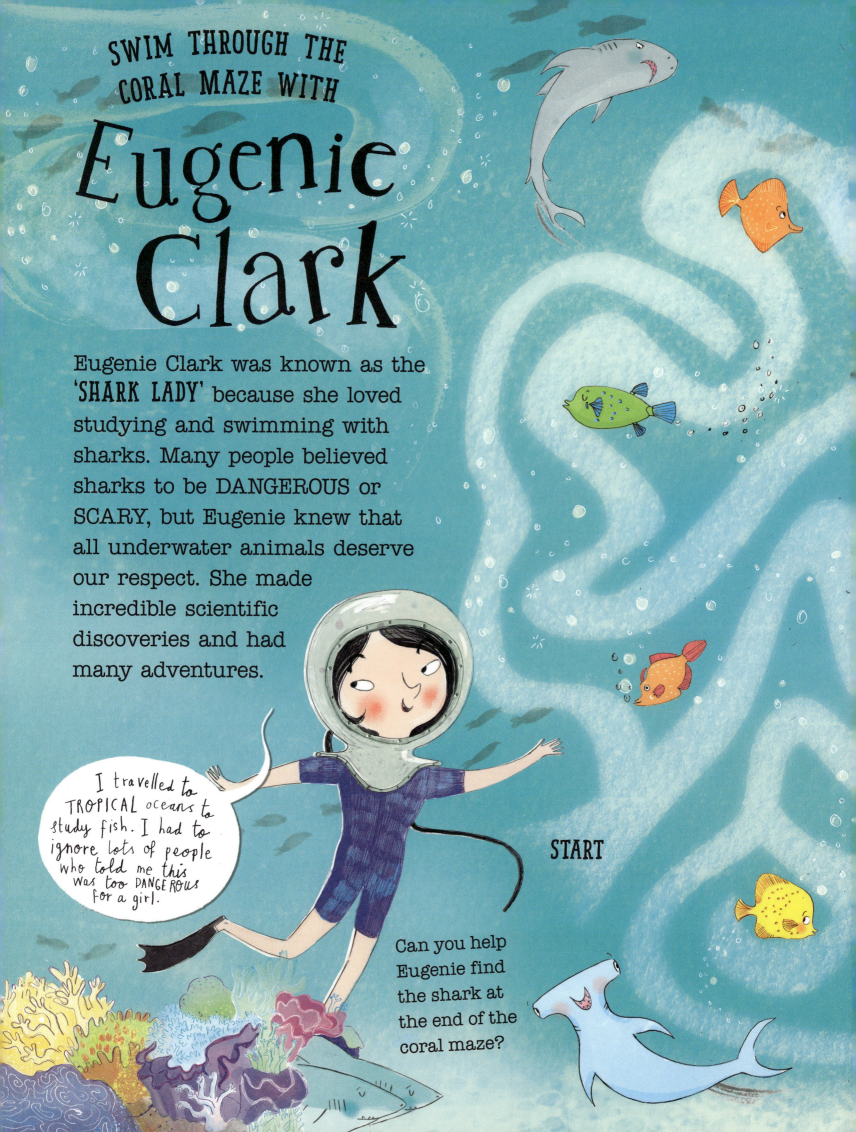

SWIM THROUGH THE CORAL MAZE WITH

Eugenie Clark

Eugenie Clark was known as the 'SHARK LADY' because she loved studying and swimming with sharks. Many people believed sharks to be DANGEROUS or SCARY, but Eugenie knew that all underwater animals deserve our respect. She made incredible scientific discoveries and had many adventures.

I travelled to TROPICAL oceans to study fish. I had to ignore lots of people who told me this was too DANGEROUS for a girl.

START

Can you help Eugenie find the shark at the end of the coral maze?

FINISH

STOP ANIMAL TESTING WITH
ANITA · RODDICK

animals in danger

SAVE THE RAINFOREST

Anita Roddick created her world-famous cosmetics business, **THE BODY SHOP**, at a time when many companies tested their products on animals. Anita did not test her products on animals and over the years she inspired other companies to work in ways that protect animals, people and the planet.

"If you do things well, do them **BETTER**. Be **DARING**, be **FIRST**, be **DIFFERENT**, be **JUST**."

REFILL HERE

Anita created shampoo, bubble bath and even make-up. If you could make your own products, what would they be? Draw them on the shelves.

Anita encouraged her customers to think about ways to help our world by hanging up posters around the shop. Design your own poster using this page.

extinct is forever

animals in danger.

BAN AGAINST ANIMAL TESTING

EDITH FARKAS

Edith Farkas was a meteorologist – a scientist who studies the weather. Edith's work showed that the ozone layer was getting thinner, which meant living things were in danger. Thanks to her work, scientists took action and today the ozone layer is in better shape.

DATE:
PLACE:

O SUN   O CLOUDS   O STORM
O SUN/CLOUDS   O RAIN   O SNOW

DETAILS:

O WARM   O COLD   O DRY   O DAMP

Be a meteorologist for a week! Keep a weather diary of each day. Is it sunny or rainy? Warm or cold? Dry or damp?

Closely observing our planet over time can reveal unexpected and important things...

DATE:
PLACE:

O SUN   O CLOUDS   O STORM
O SUN/CLOUDS   O RAIN   O SNOW

DETAILS:

O WARM   O COLD
O DRY   O DAMP

DATE:
PLACE:

O SUN   O CLOUDS   O STORM
O SUN/CLOUDS   O RAIN   O SNOW

DETAILS:

O WARM   O COLD
O DRY   O DAMP

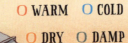

DATE:
PLACE:

○ SUN ○ CLOUDS ○ STORM

○ SUN/CLOUDS ○ RAIN ○ SNOW

DETAILS:

○ WARM ○ COLD ○ DRY ○ DAMP

DATE:
PLACE:

SUN ○ CLOUDS ○ STORM

SUN/CLOUDS ○ RAIN ○ SNOW

DETAILS:

○ WARM ○ COLD ○ DRY ○ DAMP

The ozone layer is the part of the atmosphere that protects life on Earth from the Sun's harmful rays.

DATE:
PLACE:

SUN ○ CLOUDS ○ STORM

SUN/CLOUDS ○ RAIN ○ SNOW

DETAILS:

○ WARM ○ COLD ○ DRY ○ DAMP

DATE:
PLACE:

SUN ○ CLOUDS ○ STORM

SUN/CLOUDS ○ RAIN ○ SNOW

DETAILS:

○ WARM ○ COLD ○ DRY ○ DAMP

LOOKING AT AND AFTER BEES WITH
INGEBORG BELING

Ingeborg Beling was a scientist who showed that **ALL CREATURES**, even the smallest ones, can surprise us in big ways. By studying bees, she discovered that living things have an internal clock that tells them when to eat, sleep and be active.

Ingeborg kept track of the bees she studied by painting coloured spots on them. Colour in the spots on the bees.

I painted the BEES with different coloured SPOTS so they could be easily tracked and RECOGNISED!

BUILD YOUR OWN BEE HOTEL

Create a space for lovely bees. All you need is:

- A plant pot
- Some modelling clay
- Paper straws (or hollow plant stems)

1 Place the paper straws in the plant pot, making sure they don't move. You might want to use some modelling clay to make sure they stick together.

2 Cut off the tops of the straws that are taller than the plant pot.

3 Finally, you can lay the pot down on its side in a garden, balcony or local park. Bees will come and visit!

Plant seeds for new trees with Wangari Maathai

Something must be done! The cost to the environment is too high.

When the government began to cut down forests to make room for crops worth lots of money, like coffee, Wangari Maathai took action. She started **The Green Belt Movement** to encourage people to plant new trees and tackle deforestation. Wangari sowed seeds of change and she was awarded the Nobel Peace Prize for her incredible work.

How many birds can you find on this page?

Wangari loved Kenya's lush forests, rustling leaves and streams. All this began to disappear when people started cutting down the trees! Can you help her fight deforestation by drawing your own trees on this page?

MAKE IMPORTANT ANIMAL DISCOVERIES WITH

Jane Goodall

I CLEVERLY tricked other chimps by leading them away from food so I could eat it all.

We have close family bonds and look after each other.

As a child Jane Goodall loved animals, so when she grew up she made this into a career! Jane studied chimpanzees and by doing so she saw just how similar humans and chimps are. Did you know that chimps can feel happiness, joy, pain and anger, just like us?

Jane, like many scientists, made important discoveries and kept notes. Can you keep notes on an animal of your choice? How similar is it to you? Write a list of similarities between humans and your chosen animal. Here's an example:

• I EAT FOOD FOR LUNCH

• MY CAT EATS FOOD FOR LUNCH

"The least I can do is SPEAK out for those who cannot speak for themselves."

Stick the notes stickers to the page and write your notes on them.

Design your own reusable bags with ISATOU CEESAY

When Isatou Ceesay realised how much plastic was being used in The Gambia, she came up with a clever plan ... She showed women how to recycle plastic bags into handbags and purses.

WOMEN! Your skills should not go to WASTE!

Design your own reusable bags and purses. Make them as colourful as can be!

Spot the difference with birdwatcher
FLORENCE AUGUSTA MERRIAM BAILEY

Florence Augusta Merriam Bailey lived in a time when women used bird feathers to decorate their fancy hats. She travelled around the United States to research birds and even wrote books about them, teaching people to **RESPECT** these feathered friends.

I organised nature walks with members to see wild birds.

To be a good birdwatcher, you must have an excellent eye for detail. Can you spot the difference between the birds in these pictures? There are two in each pair.

Dream of a better future with

EILEEN KAMPAKUTA BROWN AND EILEEN WANI WINGFIELD

What if something goes wrong? We don't want our land POISONED!

In the 1970s, Eileen Kampakuta Brown and Eileen Wani Wingfield led a campaign to stop the government from building a *nuclear waste dump in South Australia. They sparked conversation about how important it is to preserve the environment for our future.

* Nuclear waste is produced by nuclear power stations and can be dangerous to humans and wildlife for up to 10,000 years.

If you could dream of a better future, what would it look like? Write a list or draw a picture above.

NO TO THE RADIOACTIVE DUMP!

We may be old but that won't stop us.

Can you choose the correct route to get to the Prime Minister at Parliament House?

A B C

SAY NO to the DUMP

SYDNEY OLYMPIC GAMES

Can you spot six kangaroos on this page?

PARLIAMENT HOUSE

Make a nature collage with
THE CHIPKO MOVEMENT

In the **1960s**, logging companies chopped down countless trees in the Indian Himalayas. This caused damage to the crops and houses of people who lived there. The local women decided to peacefully protest, by hugging the trees until the loggers left. Thanks to their great courage, a temporary ban was placed on logging.

Our local trees and natural elements are precious and should be celebrated! Go outside with a friend and an adult and collect nature objects you can find on the ground. These can be leaves, twigs, feathers and more!

I will give my life before these trees are cut down! They are as important as my mother's home or 'maika'. (A place precious in Indian culture.)

Use this page to make a collage. A collage is a work of art made by putting together lots of different things.

FIND WORDS TO SAVE THE PLANET WITH MÁRIA TELKES

Can you find these fantastically great words in the word search?

Mária Telkes was a brilliant inventor who believed in the power of RENEWABLE ENERGY, such as that from the sun, waves and wind. She created the first house heated entirely using solar energy. Many houses now run on solar energy.

PLANET
SOLAR
ENERGY

RENEWABLE
FAIR TRADE
DEFORESTATION
RECYCLE

My INVENTION was a solar-heated house. I worked with some other AMAZING women to build it ...

I	W	K	Z	Q	O	O	C	W	M	G	W	D
I	E	R	X	X	R	N	D	T	X	V	M	D
R	Z	W	E	P	L	L	L	D	G	R	W	X
W	W	S	J	N	R	W	D	J	I	D	I	L
D	E	F	O	R	E	S	T	A	T	I	O	N
L	D	D	A	R	C	W	F	E	D	W	E	E
G	A	O	S	D	Y	W	A	O	U	N	F	W
X	R	U	I	L	C	T	S	B	E	Q	U	E
N	T	E	N	A	L	P	R	R	L	B	A	E
P	R	Q	W	X	E	S	G	A	Z	E	Z	S
L	I	K	J	R	T	Y	K	R	L	E	Y	N
C	A	F	I	K	Z	H	X	Q	W	O	E	V
F	F	H	N	I	M	X	O	O	X	D	S	K

BUILD YOUR OWN ROCK COLLECTION WITH URSULA MARVIN

Ursula Marvin studied space rocks in the **1950s**. She made important discoveries and it is thanks to her that we know that the moon was once a FIERY and EXPLOSIVE place, even if it's now cold. Rocks can reveal wonderful secrets!

Ursula made her brilliant discoveries by collecting rocks and observing them. Become a rock expert too by finding some rocks outside! Can you draw them in the boxes above? What do they look like?

LOOKING at the structure of rocks can help us to understand the forces that shape Earth today— like earthquakes and volcanoes.

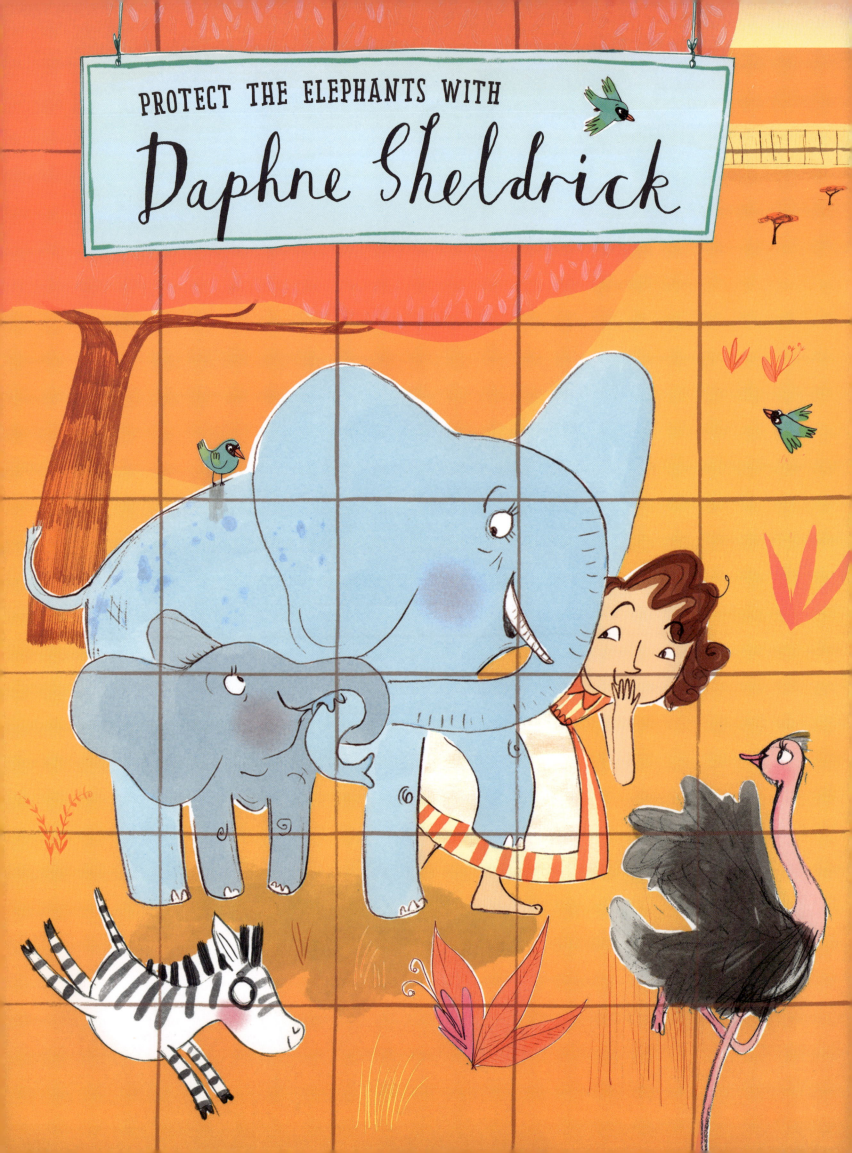

Daphne Sheldrick loved Africa's amazing wildlife, and knew how important it was to protect it. She built a National Park where she sheltered animals, especially **ELEPHANTS!** To this day, her work carries on through the charity she founded, The Sheldrick Wildlife Trust.

Copy and colour the picture of Daphne and her elephant friend, Eleanor. Use the grid as a guide.

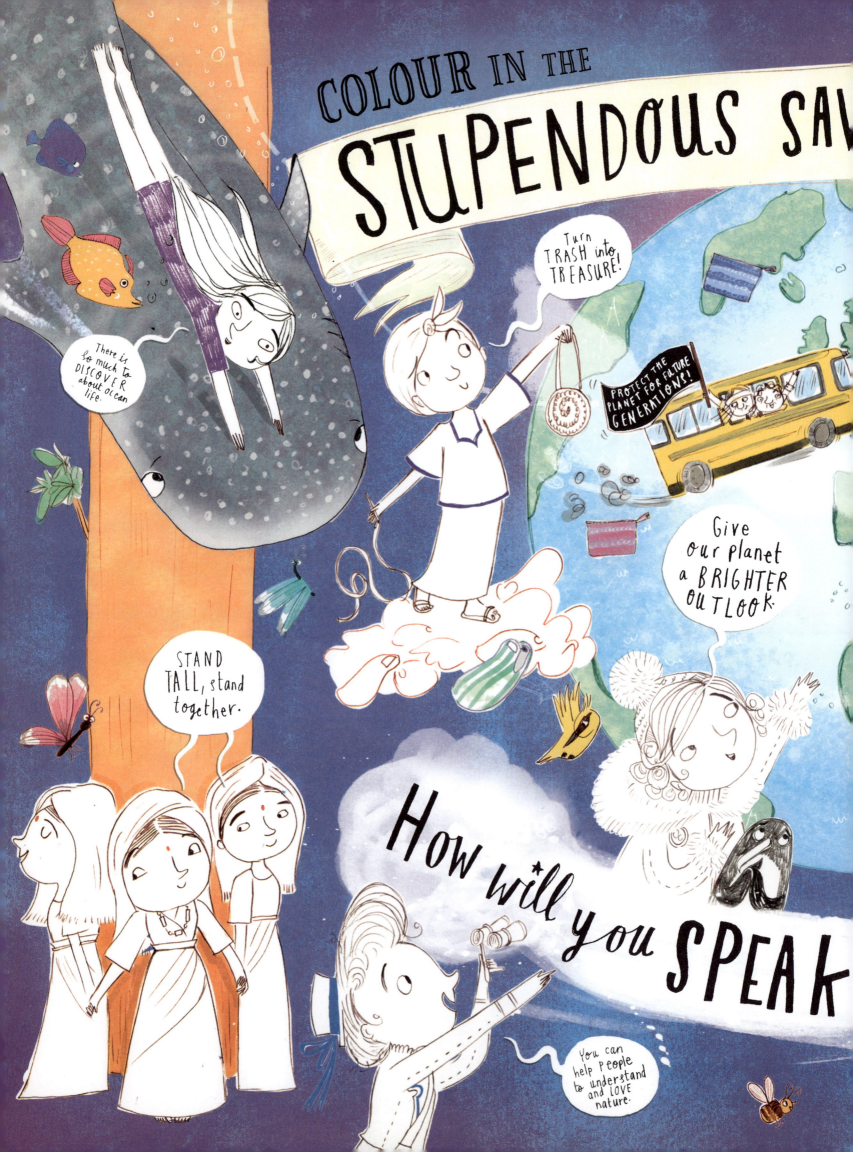

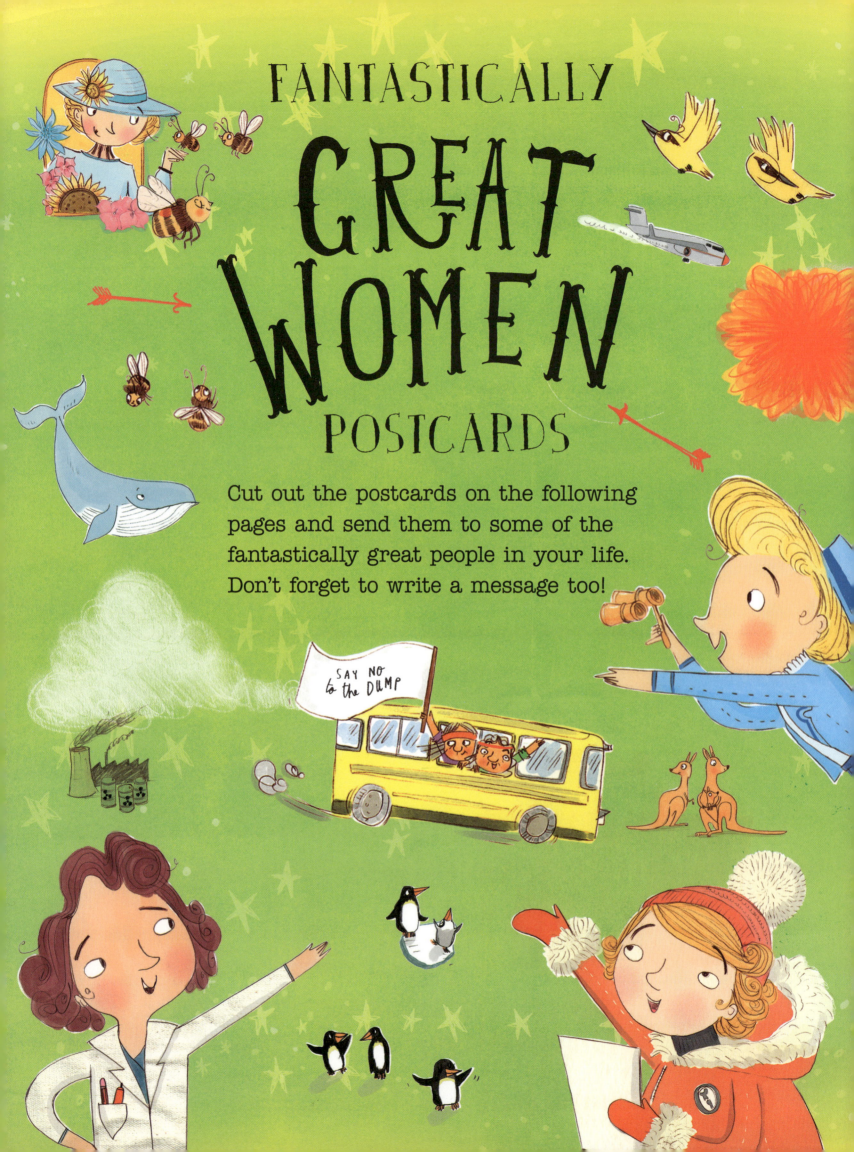

FANTASTICALLY
GREAT
WOMEN
POSTCARDS

Cut out the postcards on the following pages and send them to some of the fantastically great people in your life. Don't forget to write a message too!

SAY NO to the DUMP

Eugenie Clark

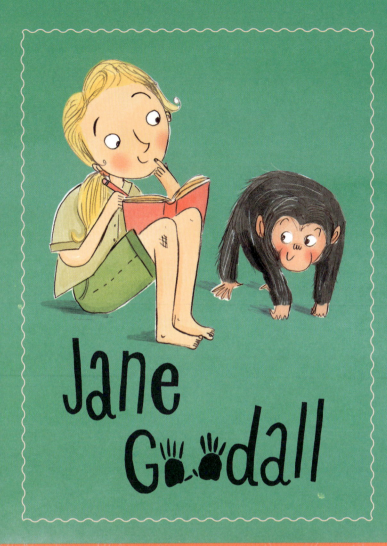

Jane Goodall

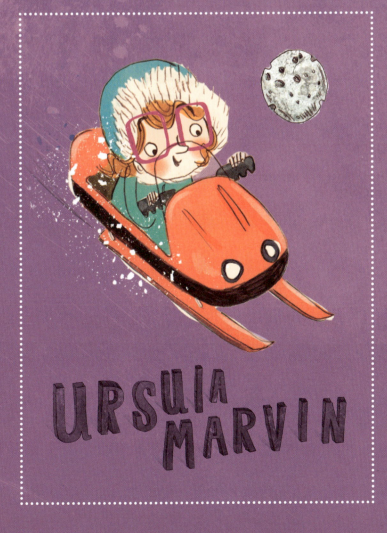

Ursula Marvin

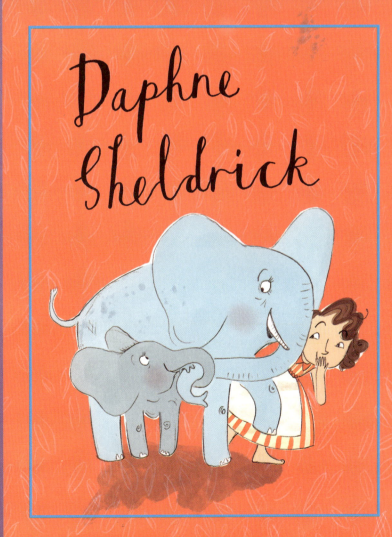

Daphne Sheldrick

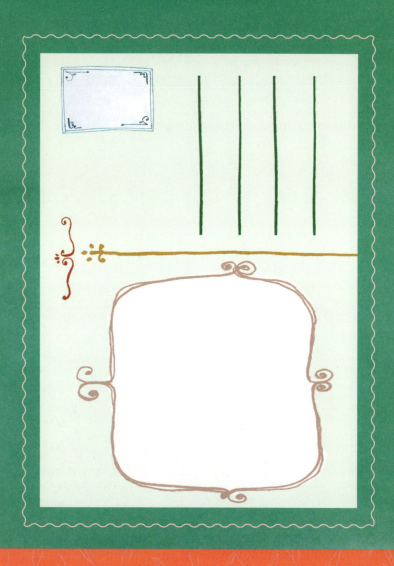

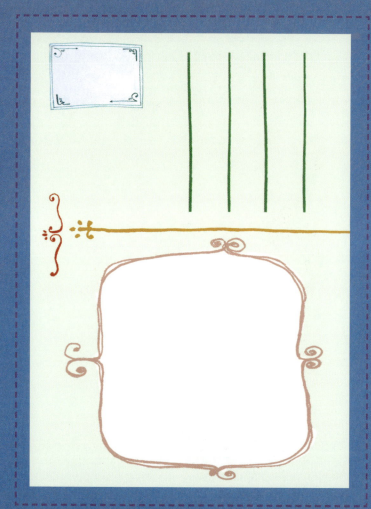

THE
CHIPKO MOVEMENT

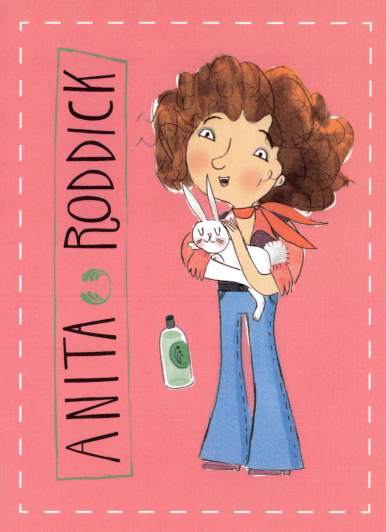

ANITA RODDICK

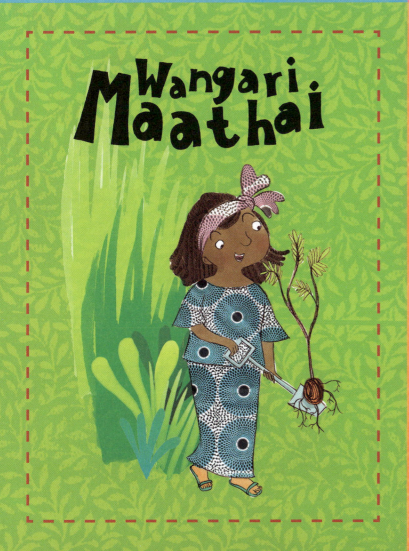

Wangari
Maathai

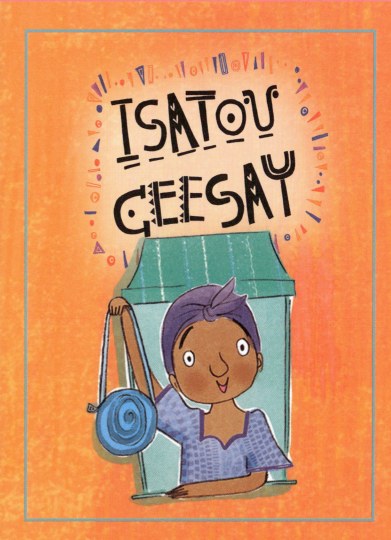

TSATOU
GEESAY

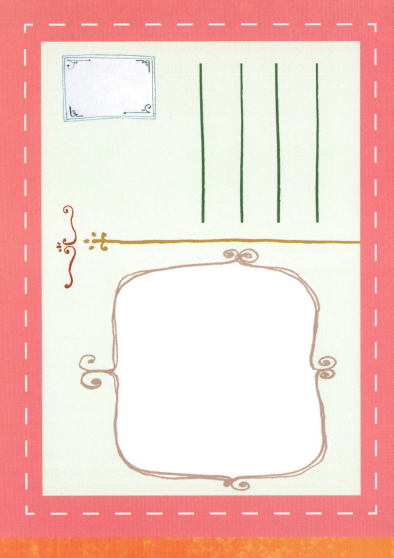
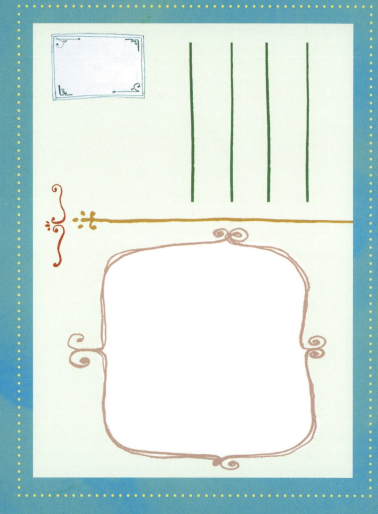

My Fantastically GREAT WOMEN

We can all save the planet by doing wonderful things! Draw someone you admire or that has made a difference to our planet in this beautiful frame.

Name:

HOW ARE YOU GOING TO SAVE THE PLANET?

The fantastically great women in this book inspired people to see that they have the power to protect our *planet's future.*

Write about what you would like to do to help save the planet.

_____

_____

_____

_____

_____

_____

_____

_____

_____

Jane Goodall